The WORLD of INSECTS

INSECT
LIFE CYCLES

Molly Aloian & Bobbie Kalman

🌳 Crabtree Publishing Company

www.crabtreebooks.com

INSECT
LIFE CYCLES

Created by Bobbie Kalman

Dedicated by Samara Parent
To Jordan DeMarco, your dad and I love you

Editor-in-Chief
Bobbie Kalman

Writing team
Molly Aloian
Bobbie Kalman

Substantive editor
Kathryn Smithyman

Editors
Kelley MacAulay
Reagan Miller
Rebecca Sjonger

Design
Margaret Amy Reiach
Samantha Crabtree (cover)
Mike Golka (series logo)

Production coordinator
Katherine Kantor

Photo research
Crystal Foxton

Consultant
Patricia Loesche, Ph.D., Animal Behavior Program,
Department of Psychology, University of Washington

Illustrations
Barbara Bedell: pages 9, 28
Margaret Amy Reiach: back cover, pages 5, 8 (larva and pupa), 25, 29
Bonna Rouse: page 8 (adult)

Photographs
James Kamstra: page 23
Robert McCaw: pages 10 (top), 12, 19 (bottom), 20 (bottom), 29
Minden Pictures: Rene Krekels/Foto Natura: page 10 (bottom)
Photo Researchers, Inc.: Dr. John Brackenbury: page 31 (top);
    Scott Camazine: page 13 (top)
Visuals Unlimited: Ken Lucas: page 25;
    Gary Meszaros: page 21;
    Bob Wilson: page 18
Other images by Brand X Pictures, Corel, Digital Vision,
    and Otto Rogge Photography

Crabtree Publishing Company

www.crabtreebooks.com   1-800-387-7650

Copyright © **2005 CRABTREE PUBLISHING COMPANY**.
All rights reserved. No part of this publication may be
reproduced, stored in a retrieval system or be transmitted in
any form or by any means, electronic, mechanical, photocopying,
recording, or otherwise, without the prior written permission
of Crabtree Publishing Company. In Canada: We acknowledge the
financial support of the Government of Canada through the Book
Publishing Industry Development Program (BPIDP) for our
publishing activities.

Cataloging-in-Publication Data
Aloian, Molly.
  Insect life cycles / Molly Aloian & Bobbie Kalman.
    p. cm. -- (The world of insects series)
  Includes index.
  ISBN-13: 978-0-7787-2343-1 (RLB)
  ISBN-10: 0-7787-2343-7 (RLB)
  ISBN-13: 978-0-7787-2377-6 (pbk.)
  ISBN-10: 0-7787-2377-1 (pbk.)
  1. Insects--Development--Juvenile literature. 2. Insects--Life cycles--
Juvenile literature. I. Kalman, Bobbie. II. Title.
  QL495.5.A46 2005
  571.8'157--dc22   2005000496
                                                          LC

**Published in
the United States**

PMB16A
350 Fifth Ave.
Suite 3308
New York, NY
10118

**Published
in Canada**

616 Welland Ave.,
St. Catharines, Ontario
Canada
L2M 5V6

**Published in the
United Kingdom**

73 Lime Walk
Headington
Oxford
OX3 7AD
United Kingdom

**Published
in Australia**

386 Mt. Alexander Rd.,
Ascot Vale (Melbourne)
VIC 3032

Contents

What are insects?

Different insects have different shapes and colors.
Some have narrow bodies. Others have round bodies.

Did you know?
Over half of all the animals on Earth are insects! Insects belong to a big group of invertebrates called **arthropods**.

Insects are animals. They are **invertebrates**. Invertebrates are animals that do not have **backbones**. A backbone is a set of bones in the middle of an animal's back.

Hard coverings

Instead of backbones, insects have hard, protective coverings on the outside of their bodies. These coverings are called **exoskeletons**. An exoskeleton covers an insect's whole body. It even covers an insect's head and legs.

4

Three body sections

An insect's body has three main sections—a head, a **thorax**, and an **abdomen**. The insect's eyes and **mouthparts** are on its head. There are also two feelers called **antennae** on an insect's head. All insects have six legs. Some insects also have wings. Legs and wings are attached to an insect's thorax. An insect's **reproductive parts** are inside its abdomen.

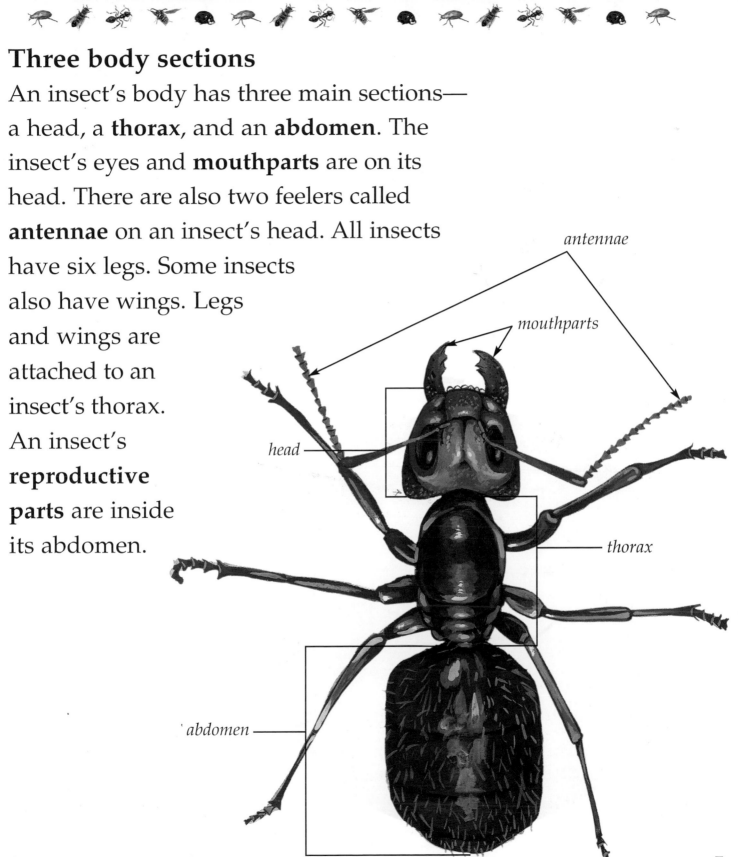

antennae

mouthparts

head

thorax

abdomen

5

What is a life cycle?

Every animal goes though a **life cycle**.
A life cycle is a set of **stages**, or changes,
in an animal's life. First, an animal is born
or hatches from an egg. The baby animal
then begins to grow. As it grows, it changes
into an adult. When it is an adult, the
animal can make babies of its own.

*The caterpillars above have hatched from eggs. They change a lot
as they grow. Eventually, the caterpillars will become butterflies.*

Changing bodies

Most insects go through **metamorphosis** during their life cycles. The word metamorphosis means "a change of **form**," or shape. After going through metamorphosis, an insect's body has changed. The insect is then an adult.

This ladybug is an adult. It has gone through metamorphosis.

This adult cicada has gone through many changes from the time it hatched from an egg to the time it became an adult.

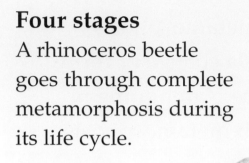

Two kinds of changes

There are two main kinds of metamorphosis. The two kinds are **complete metamorphosis** and **incomplete metamorphosis**.

Changing completely

Complete metamorphosis has four stages. The four stages are egg, **larva**, **pupa**, and adult. Beetles, moths, and butterflies go through complete metamorphosis.

Four stages

A rhinoceros beetle goes through complete metamorphosis during its life cycle.

The insect starts its life cycle inside an egg.

After hatching, the insect is called a larva.

During the third stage of its life cycle, the insect is called a pupa.

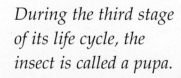

The insect is an adult in the last stage of its life cycle.

Incomplete changes

Incomplete metamorphosis has three stages. The three stages are egg, **nymph**, and adult. Dragonflies, grasshoppers, and cicadas go through incomplete metamorphosis.

Three stages

A grasshopper goes through incomplete metamorphosis during its life cycle.

The insect begins its life cycle inside an egg.

After it hatches, the insect is called a nymph.

The nymph grows and changes until it becomes an adult.

Tiny eggs

The eggs above are moth eggs. A moth larva will hatch from each egg.

Most insects start their life cycles inside eggs. Insect eggs are tiny. The biggest insect egg is only about a half-inch (1.3 cm) long! Many insect eggs are white or yellow. Others are brown or black.

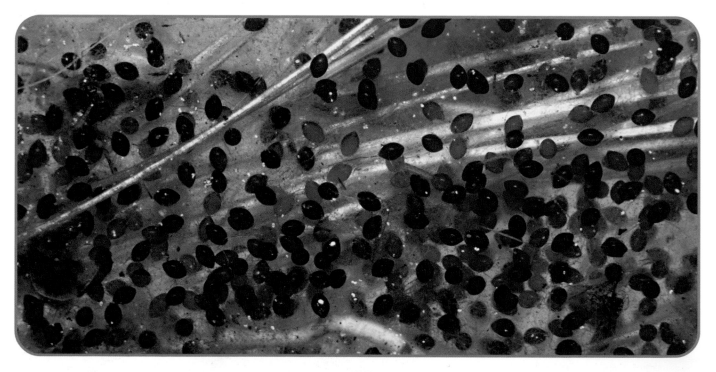

These dragonfly eggs are brown. In a few days, dragonfly nymphs will hatch from the eggs.

Time to hatch!

Most insect babies hatch in the spring or summer. During these times of the year, the weather is warm and there is plenty of food for baby insects to eat.

Breaking through

Different baby insects hatch in different ways. Some baby insects eat holes through their eggs and crawl out of the holes. Others have sharp spikes on their bodies. The spikes help the baby insects break through their eggs.

This baby Colorado potato beetle is hatching from its egg. When it has finished hatching, it will be a larva.

11

Little larvae

Insects that go through complete metamorphosis are called larvae after they hatch. Larvae do not look like their parents. Many larvae have no legs, wings, eyes, or antennae. Larvae that do not have legs cannot move from place to place.

A wood-boring beetle larva does not have legs, wings, or antennae. It cannot move very far.

This Asian ladybug larva has six legs. It can move quickly.

12

A lot of larvae

Insect larvae can have different colors, shapes, and sizes. Many larvae are tiny. Some larvae have smooth, slender bodies. Others have plump, furry bodies.

Different homes

Different larvae live in different places. Many larvae live on plants. Some larvae live on the ground. Some live in the soil, and others live inside wood. A few kinds of larvae live in water.

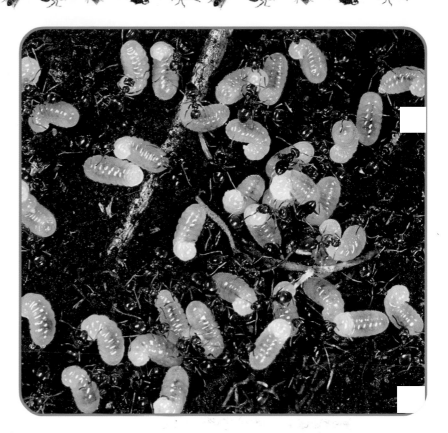

These white ant larvae live in soil. The larvae cannot move. Adult ants feed and care for the larvae.

Caterpillars are larvae. This caterpillar has a plump, furry body. It lives on the ground.

Growing quickly

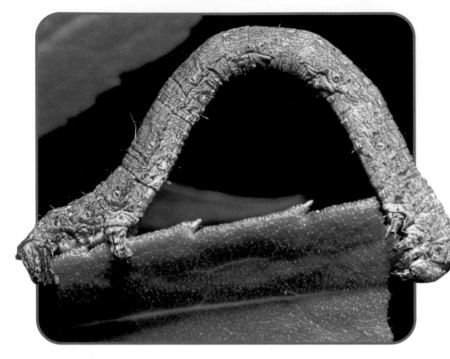

This inchworm larva is a herbivore. It is feeding on a leaf. The larva needs plenty to eat so it can grow.

Larvae must eat to stay alive. They start eating as soon as they hatch. In fact, larvae spend most of their time eating!

Foods for larvae

Different larvae eat different foods. Many larvae eat plant parts, such as leaves, roots, stems, and wood. These larvae are called **herbivores**. Some larvae eat tiny insects or small animals. Larvae that eat other animals are called **carnivores**.

The wasp larvae on the left are carnivores. Adult wasps catch insects to feed to the hungry larvae.

Shedding their exoskeletons

As larvae eat, their bodies grow. Their exoskeletons do not grow with their bodies, however. The larvae must **molt**, or shed, their exoskeletons. Molting gives the bodies of the larvae the room they need to grow bigger. Most larvae molt several times. Each time they molt, the larvae grow new, bigger exoskeletons.

This caterpillar has finished molting. Its old exoskeleton is hanging from the plant stem. The new exoskeleton has become hard around the caterpillar's body.

From larva to pupa

When a larva is ready to become a pupa, it finds a safe place. Some larvae go underground before they become pupae. Some larvae attach themselves to stems, twigs, or to the undersides of leaves. Other larvae use their mouthparts to make small holes in trees. They then crawl inside the holes and begin changing into pupae.

This anise swallowtail caterpillar is a larva. It is attaching itself to a plant stem. It will soon turn into a pupa.

Becoming pupae

Just before larvae become pupae, they molt again. After their final molts, some larvae spin tight **cocoons**, or silk cases, around themselves. Other larvae make hard cases around themselves. The cocoons and cases protect the pupae as they change into adults.

Big changes

The pupae change completely inside their cocoons and cases. The pupae develop their wings and reproductive parts. The pupae are now changing into adult insects. Many pupae do not move or eat during this stage of the life cycle.

The anise swallowtail larva is now a pupa. It looks like a green leaf. Looking like a leaf helps hide the pupa, so hungry animals will not eat it.

All grown!

When the pupae have finished changing, they **emerge**, or break out, from their cocoons and cases. They have finished complete metamorphosis. The adult insects are now able to make babies of their own.

This anise swallowtail butterfly looks very different from when it was a larva, shown on page 16.

Different bodies

The bodies of adult insects are different from the bodies they had as larvae. All adult insects have six legs. Many adults have wings.

New mouthparts

Most adult insects eat different foods than the foods they ate as larvae. Many butterfly and moth larvae have sharp mouthparts for chewing plants. As adults, the insects have long, thin mouthparts for sucking **nectar** from flowers. Nectar is a sweet liquid found in flowers.

The Asian ladybug in the middle has finished complete metamorphosis. Its body is fully formed. The pupae on either side of it are not yet adults.

curled proboscis

*An adult butterfly's long, thin mouthpart is called a **proboscis**. The butterfly curls up its proboscis when it is not sucking nectar from flowers.*

New nymphs

This shield bug nymph is in the second stage of its incomplete metamorphosis.

Insects that go through incomplete metamorphosis are called nymphs after they hatch from their eggs. Their metamorphosis is incomplete because the nymphs do not turn into pupae. There are only three stages in incomplete metamorphosis.

This spittlebug nymph protects itself from other animals by surrounding its body with a foamy liquid. It makes the liquid inside its body. The nymph hides inside the liquid.

20

Nymph bodies

Many nymphs look like small adult insects. Most nymphs have eyes, legs, and antennae. They do not have all their adult body parts, however. Nymphs do not have wings.

Hungry nymphs

To grow, nymphs need plenty of food. Some nymphs are herbivores. They suck plant juices and eat plant parts. Other nymphs are carnivores. They eat small animals. Some nymph carnivores live in water. They catch and eat animals such as tadpoles, small fish, and any insects that are in the water.

This dragonfly nymph lives in water. It does not yet have wings.

Growing wings

Nymphs molt as they grow. Most nymphs molt three or four times. Some nymphs molt between twenty and thirty times! As they molt, nymphs slowly grow wings.

Wing buds

First, nymphs develop small wings called **wing buds** on their thoraxes. Nymphs cannot use their wing buds to fly because these wings are not yet big enough. With each molt, the wing buds get bigger. When the nymphs go through their last molts, their wing buds are almost ready for flying.

Each time a dragonfly molts, its wing buds grow a little bigger.

The last molt

A nymph molts one last time before it becomes an adult. If the nymph lives in water, it crawls onto a leaf or a stem before it goes through its last molt.

Splitting open

During the molt, the nymph's exoskeleton splits open behind its head. The nymph is an adult after it has pulled itself out of the exoskeleton.

This adult dragonfly has just come out of its exoskeleton.

Adult insects

Most adult insects must wait for
their wings to dry before they can
fly. Once their wings are dry and
hard, adult insects can fly from
place to place. Adults can also
make babies of their own. The
dragonfly above is an adult.

Still the same

Many insects that go through incomplete metamorphosis eat the same foods as the foods they ate when they were nymphs. These insects do not grow different mouthparts. If a nymph had mouthparts for chewing, the adult insect will have mouthparts for chewing.

This adult stinkbug has mouthparts for sucking liquids out of the bodies of other insects. The stinkbug also had the same mouthparts when it was a nymph.

Milkweed bug nymphs and adult milkweed bugs both feed on milkweed plants.

Finding one another

Male and female insects of the same kind mate with one another.

To make babies, an adult insect must find another adult insect of the same kind with which to **mate**. To mate means to join together to make babies. Different insects have different ways of finding one another.

*Male grasshoppers, katydids, and crickets use sounds to attract females. These insects **chirp**, or make short, high-pitched sounds. They make the sounds by rubbing certain parts of their bodies together. A male grasshopper makes sounds by rubbing a leg against a wing.*

Special smells

When they are ready to mate, many female insects give off certain **scents**, or smells. The scents attract male insects to the females. Male insects use their antennae to follow the scents. Eventually, the male insects find the female insects.

The male silkworm moth has long, furry antennae. It uses its antennae to follow the scent of a female silkworm moth. After the male finds a female, the two adults will mate.

Laying eggs

After a male and a female insect mate, the female lays eggs. Most female insects lay their eggs in safe places. They lay them on the underside of leaves or bury them in sand or soil. Others lay their eggs in water. Laying eggs in safe places helps protect the eggs from animals that eat them.

This female stinkbug has laid her eggs on a leaf.

First meals

Female insects often lay their eggs on or close to the foods that the nymphs or larvae eat. For example, monarch butterflies lay their eggs on milkweed plants. When the larvae hatch, they eat the leaves of the milkweed plants.

This monarch caterpillar has hatched on a milkweed plant. It is now eating its first meal.

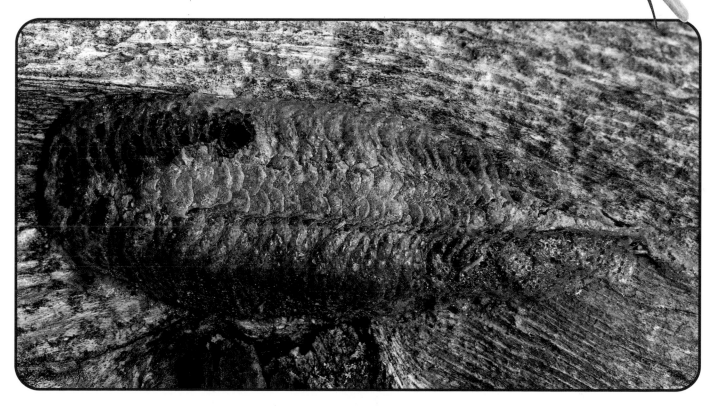

*Some insects lay their eggs inside cases called **egg cases**. The egg case of a praying mantis is shown above. The egg case protects the eggs and keeps them together.*

Big differences!

The bodies of larvae and nymphs are often very different from the bodies of adult insects. Look at the bodies of the larvae and nymphs shown on these pages and compare them to the bodies of the adult insects. How are their colors and shapes different?

This atlas moth caterpillar is a larva.

The atlas moth is now an adult. Name five ways it is different from the caterpillar above.

The insect on the left is a Colorado potato beetle larva. The insect on the right is an adult Colorado potato beetle. How is the adult different from the larva?

The insect above is a damselfly nymph. It is going through incomplete metamorphosis.

The adult damselfly looks very different from the nymph. Describe how it has changed.

31

Glossary

Note: Boldfaced words that are defined in the text may not appear in the glossary.

antennae Feelers that insects use to sense the world around them

arthropod A big group of animals with legs that bend and with bodies that are made up of sections

carnivore An animal that eats other animals

cocoon A silk case that caterpillars spin around themselves before they turn into butterflies or moths

herbivore An animal that eats plants

metamorphosis The total change of an animal's body from one form to another

molt To shed an exoskeleton and grow a larger one

mouthparts The parts on an insect's head that are used to cut, grip, and eat food

reproductive parts The adult body parts that an insect uses to join together with another insect of the same kind to make babies

Index

1 2 3 4 5 6 7 8 9 0   Printed in the U.S.A.   4 3 2 1 0 9 8 7 6 5